Published by B&H Publishing Group
Nashville, Tennessee
BHPublishingGroup.com

Custom edition published for LifeWay Christian Stores.

2 3 4 5 6 7 • 19 18 17 16 15

100
SPORTS DEVOS
FOR GIRLS

JOHN PATTON

B&H
PUBLISHING GROUP
Nashville, Tennessee

CONTENTS

ONE BODY, MANY PARTS

**For as the body is one and has many parts,
and all the parts of that body, though many,
are one body—so also is Christ.**

—1 Corinthians 12:12

What is my job as being a part of a team? Volleyball requires teamwork. For a play to be executed excellently, every player has a specific responsibility. A digger digs the spike and sets it to the setter. The setter sets up her teammate who is preparing for the spike. While she is spiking the ball, her teammates are already preparing for a block. Every player has a different job to make the play work to perfection. Such it is with us and the body of Christ. God has given each one of us special and unique gifts. Use your specific gifts in a way that makes God smile.

What is my job as being a part of a team?

_____

_____

_____

_____

_____

_____

_____

_____

_____

_____

_____

_____

_____

_____

2

GIVING 100 PERCENT

Therefore, whether you eat or drink,
or whatever you do,
do everything for God's glory.

—1 Corinthians 10:31

How do I "do everything for God's glory"? In practice or in a game when a coach does not feel like a player is giving her best effort, a coach may say, "Is that the best you got?" What she is really asking is did you play that play as hard as you can? A simple prayer that can really be prayed before every play or every drill is, "Lord, give me the strength to play this play with everything I have. Let me play this play in a way that would make You smile."

How do I "do everything for God's glory"?

_____

_____

_____

_____

_____

_____

_____

_____

_____

_____

_____

_____

_____

_____

STRONG AND COURAGEOUS

Be strong and courageous.

—Joshua 1:9

How does courage play a part in a sporting event? Being courageous does not mean you do not have any fears. Rather, it means you have the strength to face your fears and attack them, not let them conquer you. In basketball a coach may give you the challenge to guard an opponent that "seems" to be much better than you. The fear of being scored on by her can cause you to give up. The challenge is to face your fears. Facing your fears comes through a simple prayer, "Lord, give me the strength and courage to face this challenge before me and give my all to the challenge."

How does courage play a part for you in sports?

_____

_____

_____

_____

_____

_____

_____

_____

_____

_____

_____

_____

_____

_____

CHILD OF GOD

To those who are the called, loved by God the Father and kept by Jesus Christ.

—Jude 1

Do you know you are loved by God and this love comes not as a result of your performance or your success, but by the blood of His Son Jesus? How does this truth guide you in your sport? When you go to the free throw line, down by one, with no time on the clock, the fear of failure can paralyze you. But realize that whether you make the shot or miss the shot, you are still loved by God. Therefore you can take a deep breath and give your best effort. You are free to give your best because your relationship with your Father is not dependent on if you make the shot or not.

Do you know you are loved by God and this love comes by the blood of His Son Jesus?

_____

_____

_____

_____

_____

_____

_____

_____

_____

_____

_____

_____

HEART

But the LORD said to Samuel, "Do not look at his appearance or his stature . . . Man does not see what the LORD sees . . . the LORD sees the heart."

—1 Samuel 16:7

What do you see when you look in the mirror every morning? The world screams at you that what you look like is who you truly are. But God looks beneath the outer surface and looks at your heart. True beauty comes not on the outside but more on the inside. In your sport, don't focus on what you look like on the outside. No team has ever won a game because their uniforms were better than the opponent. You win games based on what is underneath the uniform. Focus on your heart more than your appearance.

FOR GIRLS

What do you see when you look in the mirror every morning?

_____

_____

_____

_____

_____

_____

_____

_____

_____

_____

_____

_____

_____

RESPECT AUTHORITY

**Everyone must submit to the governing authorities,
for there is no authority except from God,
and those that exist are instituted by God.**

—Romans 13:1

What does being a good citizen have to do with your sports team? The job of a coach is to make you better than you would be without her. Your coach is trying to get you to play at a level that you cannot achieve on your own, and she is to bring order and structure to a team. Sometimes the way she has to do this is to get after you. In basketball the coach often has to take you out of the game and have you sit on the bench to teach you what you have been doing wrong. While on the bench, you have the choice of pouting or thinking about what she said and improve on what you might have done wrong.

What does being a good citizen have to do with your sports team?

_____

_____

_____

_____

_____

_____

_____

_____

_____

_____

_____

_____

_____

DISCIPLINE

No discipline seems enjoyable at the time, but painful. Later on, however, it yields the fruit of peace and righteousness to those who have been trained by it.

—Hebrews 12:11

Have you ever heard the sentence, "The bench is the best motivator there is"? When a good coach sees that you are not playing up to your potential, she may sit you on the bench and let you watch others take your position and play. While on the bench, reflect back on if you are truly giving everything you have. Then when the opportunity comes again for you to be back on the court, give everything you have. Her "discipline" has made you a better player.

Have you ever heard the sentence, "The bench is the best motivator there is"?

_____

_____

_____

_____

_____

_____

_____

_____

_____

_____

_____

_____

_____

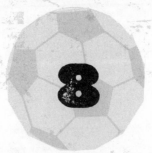

PERSEVERANCE

Let us throw off everything that hinders and the sin that so easily entangles, and let us run with perseverance the race marked out for us.

—Hebrews 12:1 (NIV)

Have you ever watched the many people running in a long race or a marathon? Often when you see a marathon taking place, you will see some runners who have costumes on while they are running. They usually wear these costumes to be funny or to promote something else. But the serious runners, those who want to win the race, have nothing extra that will slow them down. Spiritually, we are running a race called "life." There are many things that we "put on" during this race that may slow us down. Realize that the goal of your race called life is to glorify God and enjoy Him forever.

FOR GIRLS

What is your goal in this race called life?

_____

_____

_____

_____

_____

_____

_____

_____

_____

_____

_____

_____

_____

_____

TRUST

Trust in the LORD with all your heart, and do not rely on your own understanding; think about Him in all your ways, and He will guide you on the right paths.

—Proverbs 3:5–6

Trust is a belief that what I am believing in will happen. I trust that God will never leave me or forsake me, and from Scripture I know it to be true. All sports have an aspect of trust. In volleyball as one girl is hitting the ball, every other team member is getting herself in position for the next hit. So as you set the hitter, you are trusting the hitter to be in position to spike the ball. Even as the hitter is spiking the ball, the other players are positioning themselves to cover a potential block of the spike. You trust each person will do their job to make the team their very best.

Do you trust God in all you do?

_____

_____

_____

_____

_____

_____

_____

_____

_____

_____

_____

_____

_____

_____

ATTITUDE

Do nothing out of rivalry or conceit, but in humility consider others as more important than yourselves.

—Philippians 2:3

As a coach, I love seeing a great assist in basketball even more than a great shot. The assist comes because the player realizes that her teammate has a better opportunity to score than she does, so she gives up her opportunity to score and allows her teammate to score instead. What is also neat is when the one who scored quickly points her finger to the one who gave her the assist, and they both acknowledge the "team" concept of the game. How can you give "assist" to others in your life? Build up and encourage your friends when you see them do something well.

How can you give "assist" to others in your life?

_____

_____

_____

_____

_____

_____

_____

_____

_____

_____

_____

_____

_____

_____

Role Models

And what you have heard from me in the presence of many witnesses, commit to faithful men who will be able to teach others also.

—2 Timothy 2:2

Who is your hero, a woman you can look up to for an example of what you want to be someday? In tennis is it Serena or Venus Williams? In soccer it may be Abby Wambach or Mia Hamm? In your sport there is a hero that everyone looks up to and wants to be like. But who are our "heroes" on the court like in real life? How do they treat their loved ones, their fans, their teammates, their coaches? Find a role model that you can follow who sets a godly example of how a woman should treat others, and follow her example.

Who is your hero, a woman you can look
up to for an example of what you want to
be someday?

_____

_____

_____

_____

_____

_____

_____

_____

_____

_____

_____

_____

_____

PARENTS

Children, obey your parents as you would the Lord, because this is right.

—Ephesians 6:1

Often I end a practice with a "homework assignment." I tell my players that they need to go home and tell their mom and dad thanks for giving them the opportunity to play this game and that they love them. Whatever your home situation is like, you probably have a mom or dad who loves you dearly and supports you in your daily life. So often we get so busy in the day-to-day things of life that we don't stop and say thanks to those who keep us going. Your parents make great sacrifices every day to make sure you are taken care of, and most of the time it goes unnoticed. Take time today to let them know how much you appreciate them.

Have you told your parents how much you love and appreciate them?

_____

_____

_____

_____

_____

_____

_____

_____

_____

_____

_____

_____

_____

LOSING/SUFFERING

**We rejoice in our sufferings, knowing that
suffering produces endurance.**

—Romans 5:3 (ESV)

Often times "suffering" in the sports world either means injury or defeat. So why would you "rejoice" or be glad when you lose or get hurt? As I reflect back on all the sporting events I have played through life, both as a coach and as a player, the most valuable lessons I learned in life came more through my losses than my victories. These losses seem to build in me an appreciation for the game, for my teammates, for life that I did not realize when I won all the time. The "bad times" made me realize how good the good times were and motived me to give my best at every game.

FOR GIRLS

Why would you "rejoice" or be glad when you lose or get hurt?

_____

_____

_____

_____

_____

_____

_____

_____

_____

_____

_____

_____

_____

_____

BATTLE IS THE LORD'S

For the battle is the LORD's.

—1 Samuel 17:47

The context of this Scripture is when David is fighting the mighty Goliath in battle. It was a fight unto death. Thankfully our sporting events are not fighting unto death, but what we learn from David can apply to every one of our sporting events. What attitude did David have? David knew that every day he had was because God had given him that day. God is our Creator. He is the One who has made us and is the One who gives us each new day. So we give Him back each day and each game. The neat thing is it is still our job to pick up the stones and sling the rocks. So we go to practice, we play our games, all with the attitude that God who has made us is the One that works in us to slay giants.

FOR GIRLS

How is your attitude affected by your battles?

_____

_____

_____

_____

_____

_____

_____

_____

_____

_____

_____

_____

_____

CHARACTER

**Endurance produces proven character,
and proven character produces hope.**

—Romans 5:4

D. L. Moody says, "Character is what you are in the dark." What does he mean by that? Character is that hidden attribute within you that drives you to be all that you are, regardless of who is or is not watching you. Often times we may "put on a good show" because we know other people (parents, fans, coaches, players) are watching us. But your true character, who you really are, only comes out when you are in the dark and when no one is watching you. That is when your true motivation shines. Give God your character, your heart, and let Him motivate you to give your all in all.

FOR GIRLS

How does your character change when no one is watching you?

_____

_____

_____

_____

_____

_____

_____

_____

_____

_____

_____

_____

_____

_____

_____

UNSEEN VERSUS SEEN

The things we see now are here today, gone tomorrow. But the things we can't see now will last forever.

—2 Corinthians 4:18 *(The Message)*

When you see an iceberg above the surface, you are only looking at 10 percent of the size of the iceberg. There is 90 percent below the surface that is not seen when you look on the surface. The scoreboard only shows what is above the surface in a sporting event. What the scoreboard does not show is what is going on in the lives of the players and coaches and families that go much deeper than what the scoreboard says. What is behind the scoreboard are the relationships that develop through the game. Hopefully many years down the road, when you play your last competitive event, there will be friendships that you have developed with your teammates through the years. Those relationships go on long after a game is finished, and that is a good thing.

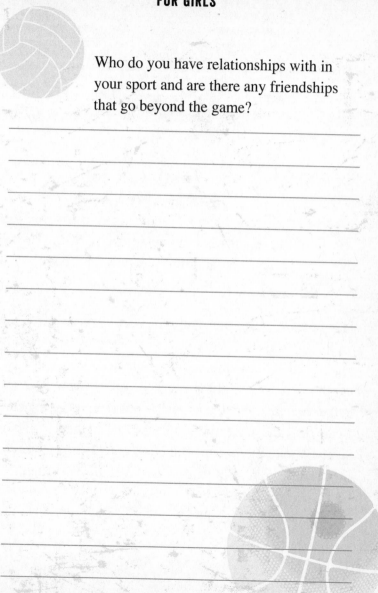

FOR GIRLS

Who do you have relationships with in your sport and are there any friendships that go beyond the game?

_____

_____

_____

_____

_____

_____

_____

_____

_____

_____

_____

_____

_____

ENCOURAGEMENT

He (Paul) gave constant encouragement, lifting their spirits and charging them with fresh hope.

—Acts 20:2 *(The Message)*

How does it make you feel when a teammate pats you on the back and encourages you after a play? Volleyball players know how important encouragement is and they do this amazingly. After every point the girls quickly gather together and say a quick word of encouragement. Even when the player didn't do well, the girls get together and build one another up. Then they quickly line up ready for the next point. But that quick word of encouragement gives the girls enough hope to keep trying and keep giving their best.

How does it make you feel when a team-mate encourages you after a play?

_____

_____

_____

_____

_____

_____

_____

_____

_____

_____

_____

_____

_____

COMPASSION

**When He saw the crowds,
He felt compassion for them.**

—Matthew 9:36

What do you see when you look across the court? In basketball the point guard comes down the court and notices (sees) what defense it is. She makes adjustments according to what she sees. But the challenge here is to look into your teammates and see beyond the surface. When a teammate makes a mistake, you see how they feel like a failure. This may be the perfect time for you to encourage them. Jesus saw the crowds and had compassion on them, and He healed the sick. You may not be able to heal the sick, but you can reach out and help your teammate who may be hurting.

What do you do when you see a teammate
hurting?

_____

_____

_____

_____

_____

_____

_____

_____

_____

_____

_____

_____

_____

_____

SLING SHOT (TRUST IN GOD)

David put his hand in his bag, took out a stone, slung it, and hit the Philistine on his forehead.

—1 Samuel 17:49

What are the stones God has given you? Here the stones represent the ability or tools God has given you to face the world. From the world's perspective, five stones and a sling shot were not enough to face the mighty giant Goliath and his armor. Yet God knew that as long as David trusted in the Lord, it was all he needed. David learned a great lesson that day. The battle is the Lord's, yet David still had to pick up the stones and sling them at Goliath. God gives you the strength to play, yet it is up to you to go and play. So go and play in His strength.

FOR GIRLS

What are the stones God has given you?

_____

_____

_____

_____

_____

_____

_____

_____

_____

_____

_____

_____

_____

_____

SPEAK TRUTH IN LOVE

Speaking the truth in love.

—Ephesians 4:15 (NLT)

What does speaking the truth in love have to do with sports? Communication can take on many forms other than just talking. You can communicate with a high five, a pat on the back, a smile of encouragement, or whatever. But you also have the opportunity to communicate with your words. And this verse challenges us to sometimes speak hard words to our teammates, but to speak them in love. One of the struggles in any sport is to give your best every minute of the game and practice. When you see a teammate not giving their best, try to encourage them with words to make them give their best. Don't beat them down, rather build them up and challenge them to give their all; as you give your all.

What does speaking the truth in love have to do with sports?

_____

_____

_____

_____

_____

_____

_____

_____

_____

_____

_____

_____

_____

PRACTICE

What you have learned and received and heard and seen in me—practice these things.

—Philippians 4:9 (ESV)

How do you get better at your sport? Practice, practice, practice. I can still hear my father telling me, "Practice makes perfect" or statements like, "You play like you practice." Practice is an inner discipline that makes you better prepared for your game. Your attitude about how you practice will prepare you for the game. When you go to the foul line with no time remaining and you are down by one, the time and effort you spent practicing those free throws will give you a peace knowing that you are prepared to give your best.

How do you get better at your sport?

_____

_____

_____

_____

_____

_____

_____

_____

_____

_____

_____

_____

_____

_____

GOALS/AIM

Whether we are at home or away, we make it our aim to be pleasing to Him.

—2 Corinthians 5:9

Why do you play your sport? What motivates you to get up and practice every day? Some people play sports only to please their parents or to please someone else. Some people play because they have to, not because they enjoy it. But as a Christian, we should play our sport with the goal to please Jesus. But the neat thing about pleasing Jesus is that He doesn't really care if we win or lose, He cares about how we play when we play. He wants us to play with all our heart. He is concerned about how we treat each other.

Why do you play your sport?

_____

_____

_____

_____

_____

_____

_____

_____

_____

_____

_____

_____

_____

_____

23

LORD'S STRENGTH

You come against me with a dagger, spear, and sword, but I come against you in the name of Yahweh of Hosts.

—1 Samuel 17:45

How do you face opponents who may seem bigger, stronger, and better than you? David, when he was a youth, had to face such an opponent, but his battle was not just a game, it was a battle for life. And David teaches us that our real strength is not in our own ability, but in the Lord. God is the One who has given you the body you have. He is the One who gives you the strength to face each day. A simple prayer before each sporting event and even all during the event is, "Lord, thank You for giving me my ability. Everything I have is Yours. I give it back to You and want to honor You by giving You all I have. Amen."

FOR GIRLS

How do you face opponents who may seem
bigger, stronger, and better than you?

_____

_____

_____

_____

_____

_____

_____

_____

_____

_____

_____

_____

_____

HUMILITY

**Make your own attitude that of Christ Jesus,
. . . He humbled Himself.**

—Philippians 2:5, 8

How does being humble play a role in being a good athlete? *Humility* is "strength in perfect submission." A great example of humility is a Thoroughbred horse. As strong and massive as the horse is, it is directed by the little twitch of the jockey directing it. Humility is not simply letting the opponent beat you; it is giving every ounce of your strength to your sport, yet being under perfect control while you play. Humility is acknowledging that everything you have, every breath you take, is only because God has given you your strength and even your next breath.

How does being humble play a role in being a good athlete?

_____

_____

_____

_____

_____

_____

_____

_____

_____

_____

_____

_____

_____

ANXIETY

Cast all your anxiety on him because he cares for you.

—1 Peter 5:7 (NIV)

In any close game, there are going to be highs and lows that come on both sides. Sometimes the momentum is in your favor and it feels like the ball is rolling your way. Yet there are other times when it feels like everything is going against you and you are not getting the breaks you need to win the game. During the heat of the game, pray to God and give Him your concerns. Your prayer may be, "Lord, give me wisdom or give me strength." God is with you through the highs and lows because He cares for you. He is concerned about what happens to you, so give Him your concerns.

What are your concerns that keep you from doing your best?

_____

_____

_____

_____

_____

_____

_____

_____

_____

_____

_____

_____

_____

SELF-CONTROL

You must not follow a crowd in wrongdoing.

—Exodus 23:2

Sporting events can be very emotional. Fans can get fired up about a bad call by an official, and the next thing you know they are ready to fight the opponents or the officials. But as an athlete, keep your cool and don't follow your peers or even your fans if they are setting a negative tone. Self-control is a very important characteristic to have in sports. Keep your mind focused on controlling yourself and don't allow others to determine how you will play.

Have you ever lost control or seen someone else get out of control?

_____

_____

_____

_____

_____

_____

_____

_____

_____

_____

_____

_____

_____

ENDURANCE

**Let us run with endurance the race
that lies before us.**

—Hebrews 12:1

What is endurance? *Endurance* is pushing through the course to achieve the set goal. In cross country, a runner knows the course before her and paces herself to endure through the whole race. Usually on a cross country course there are valleys and hills. Endurance is pushing yourself up the hills even when you feel you are too tired to take another step. Every sport takes on its own form of endurance, the ability to push through to the end. As we fix our eyes on Jesus we find the strength to see the course to the end.

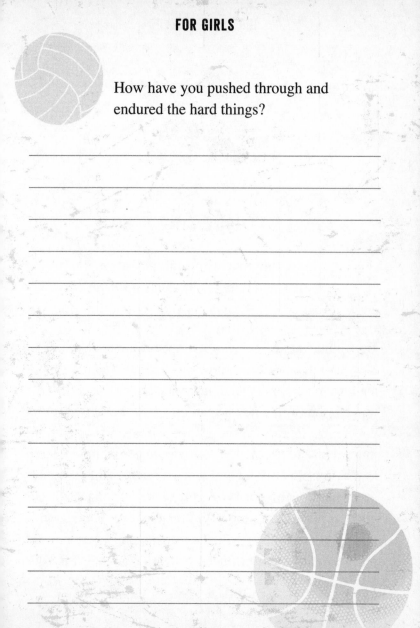

How have you pushed through and
endured the hard things?

_____

_____

_____

_____

_____

_____

_____

_____

_____

_____

_____

_____

_____

LOVE ONE ANOTHER

**Love one another with brotherly affection.
Outdo one another in showing honor.**

—Romans 12:10 (ESV)

One of the greatest things about team sports is learning to play in a way that truly shows love to your teammates. A team sport is saying that more are better than one. Six volleyball players are better than one. Five basketball players can do more than one. Nine softball players can do more than one. So love comes when all members learn to play unselfishly and in a way that makes the team better. When I learn that loving my teammates means I will give my very best effort, it makes the team better; and it makes me better. Give your best effort today, and may the motivation for that effort be because you care for your teammates.

How have you demonstrated love for your teammates?

_____

_____

_____

_____

_____

_____

_____

_____

_____

_____

_____

_____

_____

_____

POWER

**Now to Him who is able to do above
and beyond all that we ask or think according
to the power that works in us.**

—Ephesians 3:20

A Christian has a secret power that those who do not believe in Jesus do not have. That power is the Holy Spirit who lives in you, and He gives you strength and power to make you the best you can be. When I was at my summer camp and was training for my sport, there was a three-mile run around the campus that ended with a long up hill run. At the end of the run, there was a large cross. I would fix my eyes on the cross as I ran up that last hill and find the strength within me to finish the race. That strength to give my best came from God living inside me.

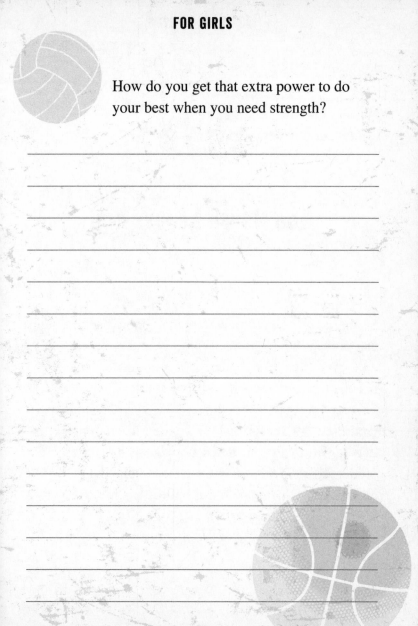

How do you get that extra power to do your best when you need strength?

_____

_____

_____

_____

_____

_____

_____

_____

_____

_____

_____

_____

_____

GOD NEVER LEAVES YOU

I, the God of Israel, will not forsake them.

—Isaiah 41:17

Sometimes the fear of messing up or doing bad in a game can prevent you from really trying hard to succeed. You are scared that if you mess up, you will be put on the bench or treated unkindly by your coach. This verse gives great comfort and freedom to you as you play your sport. God does not accept or love you based on your performance. He loves you based on what His Son Jesus did on the cross. Therefore you are free to play with all your heart because messing up can't affect His love for you.

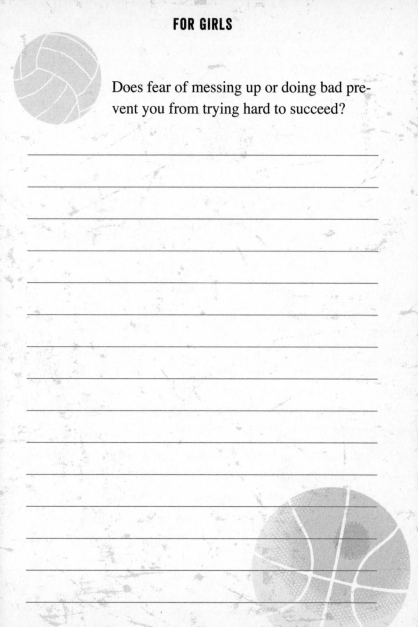

Does fear of messing up or doing bad prevent you from trying hard to succeed?

SELF-CONTROL

For God gave us a spirit not of fear but of power and love and self-control.

—2 Timothy 1:7 (ESV)

Do you ever get upset or lose your control at a game? In basketball the lead can change within seconds. One second you are so happy because you are winning, and within seconds the other team can score and you are suddenly extremely upset. Your emotions are a big part of your sport. Giving everything you have means giving your emotions as well. God knows this and gives you the power and strength to control your emotions positively and use your emotions to make you a better player.

Do you ever get upset or lose your control
at a game?

_____

_____

_____

_____

_____

_____

_____

_____

_____

_____

_____

_____

_____

_____

TWO ARE BETTER THAN ONE

Two are better than one because they have a good reward for their efforts.

—Ecclesiastes 4:9

Have you ever been "double teamed" in a basketball game? A double team happens when the coach needs to stop a certain player, so she will put two players on that one person. It is hard for that one person to defeat the double team. The strategy behind a double team is that two are better than one. Two people working together can do more that one can do on her own. Team sports require individuals to work together to become better. In life we are in relationship with one another, and we need to learn how to work together. Learn how to be a team player.

Have you ever been "double teamed" in a basketball game?

_____

_____

_____

_____

_____

_____

_____

_____

_____

_____

_____

_____

_____

RUNNING WELL

You were running well. Who prevented you from obeying the truth?

—Galatians 5:7

What things prevent you from playing your best? As you go through a season, there are many things that can hinder or distract you from being the best you can be. Some of these things are out of your control, like an injury or a sickness. But many of the things are in your control. Your attitude and your effort are in your control. As the season goes along, it is easy to lose focus and the drive that motivated you early in the season. Keep your eyes on the goal, and when outside things hinder you or keep you from giving your best, reset your gaze on the goal. For your spiritual goal always keep your eyes focused on Jesus.

What things prevent you from playing your best?

_____

_____

_____

_____

_____

_____

_____

_____

_____

_____

_____

_____

_____

_____

HONESTY

The Lord hates cheating and delights in honesty.
—Proverbs 11:1 *(The Living Bible)*

Most sports have officials who try to make sure the game is played with each side having an equal chance of winning the event. But there are some sports, like tennis and golf, where you are your own "official." In golf you are not supposed to move your ball from the original spot because it may be giving you an advantage over your opponent. In tennis you are your own line judge, meaning if you see the ball hit on the line or inside the line, the honest thing to do is call it in. Honesty is something God values highly because it is true and right. Cheating is giving you an unfair advantage. Play with honesty and integrity and you will have peace about the outcome.

FOR GIRLS

What is your attitude about cheating?

_____

_____

_____

_____

_____

_____

_____

_____

_____

_____

_____

_____

_____

_____

35

TRUST IN HORSES OR CHARIOTS?

**Some trust in chariots and some in horses,
but we trust in the name of the LORD our God.**

—Psalm 20:7

What do you ultimately trust in? Is it your own strength or your own speed or ability? In the Bible we find that our ultimate strength comes from the Lord, the maker of heaven and earth. God is the One who has made everything in this world. He is the One who gives us each new day. He is the One who gave us the bodies and ability we have to play our sport. It is easy to lose sight of this and think that it is all about you, but never lose sight of the fact that God is the One who gives you everything you have. Trust in Him.

What do you ultimately trust in?

_____

_____

_____

_____

_____

_____

_____

_____

_____

_____

_____

_____

_____

_____

36

GOD IS ON YOUR SIDE

**Then this message came to Jeremiah:
"I am the Lord, the God of all mankind;
is there anything too hard for me?**

—Jeremiah 32:26–27 *(The Living Bible)*

I find that the harder the opponent I am going up against, the more I pray. And on the opposite side, I find that I often do not pray as much when my opponent is weaker. The prophet Jeremiah lived in a tough time when Israel was up against some very strong enemies. God's message to Jeremiah was to remember and believe that as long as God was on his side, anything was possible. As in how you play sports, remember that as long as you are giving everything to God, nothing is impossible.

When things get tough, do you pray or do you just give up?

_____

_____

_____

_____

_____

_____

_____

_____

_____

_____

_____

_____

_____

TESTS AND TRIALS

Consider it a great joy, my brothers, whenever you experience various trials, knowing that the testing of your faith produces endurance.

—James 1:2

Honestly, how would it be if you won every game you played by a large margin? If you did, you would find that you would quickly lose heart and intensity in playing the game as hard as you can play. The tests and challenges come when the opponent is equal or even better than you. It makes you try harder and give everything you have. When you are the underdog, often you try harder and learn more about yourself and the game because you are giving more of yourself to the game.

Honestly, how would it be if you won every game you played by a large margin?

_____

_____

_____

_____

_____

_____

_____

_____

_____

_____

_____

_____

_____

_____

DEVELOPING CHARACTER

The testing of your faith produces endurance. But endurance must do it's complete work, so that you may be mature and complete, lacking nothing.

—James 1:3–4

In the heat of the game when you are giving everything you have, your true character seems to come out. Sports are a great tool that teach you how to give everything you have to a certain thing, your sport. But what a valuable lesson to learn about life and your faith. Give God everything!

Do you feel you give everything to your team when you play sports?

_____

_____

_____

_____

_____

_____

_____

_____

_____

_____

_____

_____

_____

IRON SHARPENS IRON

Iron sharpens iron, and one man sharpens another.
—Proverbs 27:17

Often times a coach will alternate two players at a position, subbing each one in an out of the game. When the one player does well, it makes the other player step up and do well also because she knows that if she doesn't, she may lose her position. So the success of one also breeds the success of the other. It would be easy to silently hope your teammate doesn't do well so you can have her position, but realize that her success is really making you a better player as well, and this makes the team stronger.

Who on your team makes you a better player?

GLORY OF GOD—MAN FULLY ALIVE

**A thief comes only to steal and to kill and to destroy.
I have come so that they may have life
and have it in abundance.**

—John 10:10

There was a godly man who lived in the third century who said, "the glory of God is man fully alive." One of Satan's goals is for you to go through life halfheartedly, not really trying nor giving much effort to anything. He simply wants you to exist and waste your life away. But Jesus is just the opposite. He wants you to live your life full speed; to give everything you have at every practice and every game. Living life and playing every sport full speed puts a smile on God's face because He knows that you are using the gifts He has given you to the maximum capacity.

How do you use the gifts God has given
you in sports and at home?

_____

_____

_____

_____

_____

_____

_____

_____

_____

_____

_____

_____

_____

_____

I WANT TO KNOW CHRIST

I want to know Christ and the power of his resurrection and the fellowship of sharing in his sufferings.

—Philippians 3:10 (NIV)

How do you come to know someone and what does that have to do with sports? You come to know someone by spending time with that person, over and over again. You don't come to know someone by being with her one time. Whatever sport you play, you will spend time with your teammates, and they will likely become some of the best friends of your life. You will be with them through the wins and the losses, through the hard practices and tough times. As you begin to know them, share your heart and life with them and experience the beauty of coming to know others, an incredible blessing from God our Father.

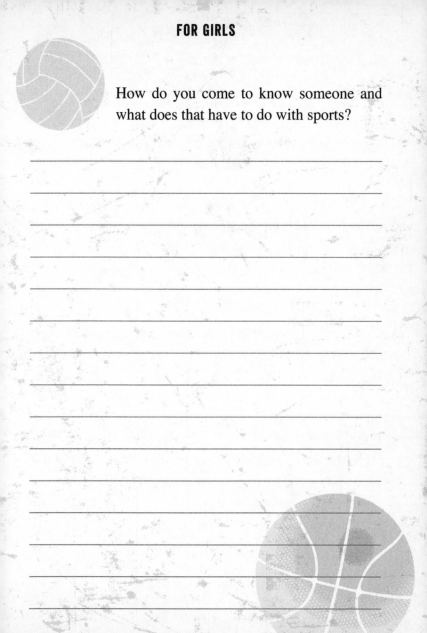

How do you come to know someone and what does that have to do with sports?

_____

_____

_____

_____

_____

_____

_____

_____

_____

_____

_____

_____

_____

HONOR YOUR PARENTS

Honor your father and your mother.

—Exodus 20:12

God is a God of order and structure, not chaos. And when God was designing the family and what structure it would be, He had order and design in it for a reason, because that worked best. God has placed your mom and dad over you because they will protect, provide, guide, and love you through every stage of your life. Honoring them is giving them the credit they deserve for raising you through this thing called "life." In your sporting event, honoring your parents is playing in a respectful and honorable way in each practice and every game.

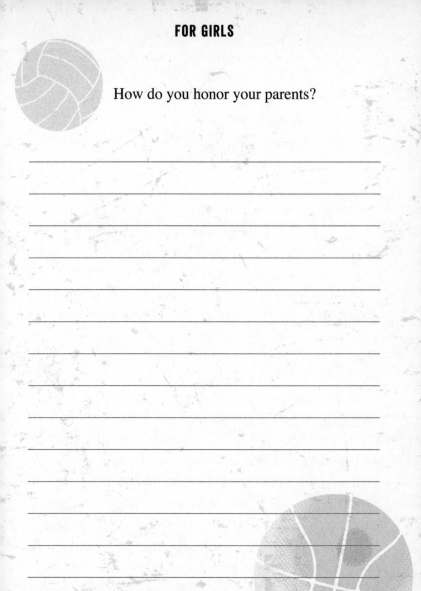

FOR GIRLS

How do you honor your parents?

_____

_____

_____

_____

_____

_____

_____

_____

_____

_____

_____

_____

_____

_____

DO NOT USE BAD LANGUAGE

No foul language is to come from your mouth, but only what is good for building up someone in need, so that it gives grace to those who hear.

—Ephesians 4:29

The beautiful thing about a game is that if played well, it demands you give everything you have to succeed. When you give everything you have, sometimes you come up short or things don't go the way you hoped they would. At that point it is very easy to let your emotions rule and you end up saying or yelling something that is not positive. God is the One who has given us language as a way to communicate. As Christians we are to use our language in a way that builds up and encourages our teammates, not tear them or our opponent down.

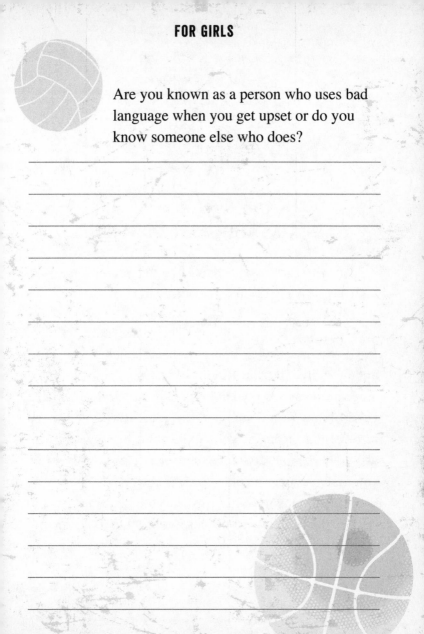

Are you known as a person who uses bad language when you get upset or do you know someone else who does?

_____

_____

_____

_____

_____

_____

_____

_____

_____

_____

_____

_____

_____

_____

MAINTAIN SELF-CONTROL

**In the same way, encourage the young men
to be self-controlled.**

—Titus 2:6

Have you ever had to hold your hand up when you commit a foul in basketball? In the old days, when you fouled you would have to hold your hand up so the scorers table would know you committed the foul. If you held it up in rebellion or anger, you could get a technical foul as well. The simple act of raising your hand calmly when you fouled taught the players self-control. No matter how bad the call may have been, you, as the player, learned to respect the official and not lose your temper. As intense as your game may be, you must continue to maintain your self-control.

FOR GIRLS

How do you maintain self-control during an intense game?

_____

_____

_____

_____

_____

_____

_____

_____

_____

_____

_____

_____

_____

_____

REMEMBERED WELL

I will also make every effort that you may be able to recall these things at any time after my departure.

—2 Peter 1:15

How do you want to be remembered as an athlete? There may be certain plays or games that you remember for a long time, but more important than the games or plays is the legacy you leave behind. As a coach, the players that I remember are the ones that gave 100 percent every time they showed up for practice or the game. They hustled and their hustle made the coaches believe in them. Learn how to play with all your strength, all your mind, and all your heart, and you will be remembered by your coach as one of those gals who laid it all on the court.

How do you want to be remembered as an athlete?

_____

_____

_____

_____

_____

_____

_____

_____

_____

_____

_____

_____

_____

KNOCKED DOWN—GET BACK UP

**We are persecuted but not abandoned;
we are stuck down but not destroyed.**

—2 Corinthians 4:9

In every sporting event, there are times when you get behind or you have your back against the wall. It looks like defeat and the game is over. But you learn to keep on going and to get back into the game. It is like being knocked down.

But you learn to get back up and get ready for the next play. There will be times in life when you are knocked down, when things just don't go the way you want them to go. Realize that God is with you and He will give you the strength to get back up and face another day.

FOR GIRLS

What happened when you were "knocked down" in a game or when life became hard?

_____

_____

_____

_____

_____

_____

_____

_____

_____

_____

_____

_____

BE STRONG IN THE LORD

"Even so, be strong, Zerubbabel"—this is the LORD's declaration. "Be strong, Joshua son of Jehozadak, high priest. Be strong, all you people of the land"— this is the LORD's declaration. "Work! For I am with you"—the declaration of the LORD of Hosts.

—Haggai 2:4

Courage is the ability to face your fears instead of running from them. Sometime you will face opponents who are far superior than you are, and the task of standing up to them is daunting. How do you face such opponents? We are to take courage, not in ourselves but in the fact that God is with us and He will never leave us or abandon us. We find the courage to face the opponent comes from God, who is strong and faithful. So take courage because God is with you.

What is your attitude toward tough opponents?

_____

_____

_____

_____

_____

_____

_____

_____

_____

_____

_____

_____

_____

RESPECT FOR OFFICIALS

You are to rise in the presence of the elderly and honor the old. Fear your God; I am Yahweh.

—Leviticus 19:32

Respect for the older generation seems to almost be a lost trait; but those who love and revere the Lord will show respect to your elders. Officials will make bad calls. They are human, just like you, and they will mess up just like you. But when they mess up or make a bad call (in your opinion), you can still treat them with respect and honor even if you disagree with their call. Don't treat officials as enemies or someone out to harm you. Treat them with kindness and respect and honor as you play your sport. May your good behavior toward the officials be a testimony of your relationship with Jesus Christ.

What is your attitude toward the officials
and coaches when they mess up?

_____

_____

_____

_____

_____

_____

_____

_____

_____

_____

_____

_____

_____

PERFECT LOVE DRIVES OUT FEAR

There is no fear in love; instead, perfect love drives out fear, because fear involves punishment. So the one who fears has not reached perfection in love.

—1 John 4:18

What drives you to play the best you can play? Is it fear or love? Do you fear the coach yelling at you or treating you with shame and guilt, or does love motivate you to play your best? Some coaches try to motivate you by making you feel bad or unimportant, but other coaches get you to play your best by building you up. The greatest motivator in this world is love. Learn to play the game with love as the motivating factor that makes you the best you can be.

What drives you to play the best you can play?

_____

_____

_____

_____

_____

_____

_____

_____

_____

_____

_____

_____

_____

50

MOUNT UP WITH WINGS LIKE EAGLES

"But they who wait for the LORD shall renew
their strength; they shall mount up with wings
like eagles; they shall run and not be weary;
they shall walk and not faint.

—Isaiah 40:31 (ESV)

Where does your strength come from? As you push yourself through the discipline of your sport, realize that more important than your self-discipline is your trust in God who gives you every breath you take. As we look to God for our strength, there will be times when we feel like flying like eagles; other times when we run without growing tired, and still other times when all we can do is walk and not pass out. But through every season of life, God promises to be there for us and will never abandon or forsake us.

Where does your strength come from?

_____

_____

_____

_____

_____

_____

_____

_____

_____

_____

_____

_____

_____

SHAME

Keeping our eyes on Jesus, the source and perfecter of our faith, who for the joy that lay before Him endured a cross and despised the shame.

—Hebrews 12:2

What is your greatest nightmare about a sporting event? You are fouled at the buzzer and are down by two. You have to go to the foul line and hit both free throws to send the game into overtime. You miss and the game is over. You pull your shirt over your head and wish you could just crawl up in a hole and hide. But this verse tells us that Jesus has carried the shame for us so we don't have to. Our good standing before God is not based on whether we can hit the free throw or not. We are free to try because He has carried our shame.

What is your greatest nightmare about a sporting event?

CARRY YOUR LOAD

For each person will have to carry his own load.
—Galatians 6:5

Even though you may be in a team sport, you still have individual responsibility and your team is counting on you to do your duties to the best of your ability. Understand your load and carry your load well.

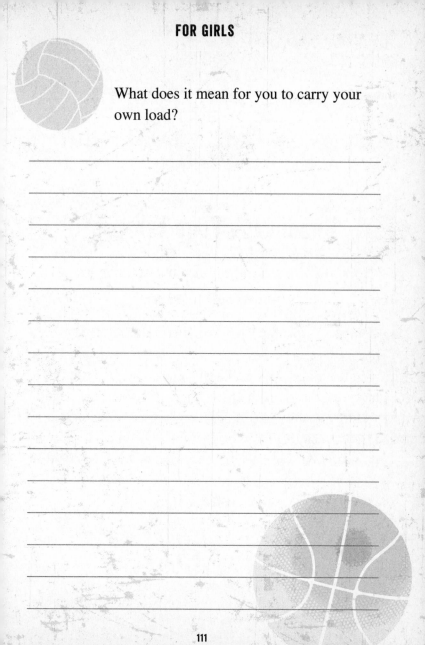

What does it mean for you to carry your own load?

_____

_____

_____

_____

_____

_____

_____

_____

_____

_____

_____

_____

_____

_____

ENCOURAGE YOUR TEAMMATE

Work at getting along with each other and with God.
—Hebrews 12:14 *(The Message)*

Competition within a team can make the whole team better because it pushes every member on the team. When your teammate does well, learn to encourage her and build her up. Confess any pride or jealousy you may have in selfishly wanting the praise and glory to go to you instead of your teammate. As you learn to encourage others who do well, you will begin to enjoy the team aspect of your game. Find more joy and contentment over the team's success than your own individual success.

How well do the members of your team
get along and encourage one another?

_____

_____

_____

_____

_____

_____

_____

_____

_____

_____

_____

_____

_____

_____

WEEDS OF BITTERNESS

Make sure that no one falls short of the grace of God and that no root of bitterness springs up, causing trouble and by it, defiling many.

—Hebrews 12:15

Your sport will have some incredible highs, but it will also have some incredible lows. From time to time, you may find yourself on a team that has a hard time winning. Losing is not fun for anyone, but there are lessons we can learn from losing. Do not let a poor attitude sneak in and discourage you and your teammates. Find the good in every loss. Find what you can learn positively from every negative thing that happens, and don't let weeds of bitterness sneak in and destroy your team.

What is your attitude when you are on a losing team?

_____

_____

_____

_____

_____

_____

_____

_____

_____

_____

_____

_____

_____

_____

CREATED IN THE IMAGE OF GOD

Then God said, "Let us make man in Our image, according to Our likeness. They will rule the fish of the sea, the birds of the sky, the livestock, all the earth, and the creatures that crawl on the earth."

—Genesis 1:26

We are created in the image of God, meaning every day we live we have the opportunity and responsibility to live for His glory. Being created in His image means we are a *created person*. *Created* means every day we live, we live because God gave us this day. *Person* means we can choose what we do this day. Today you choose how hard you are going to work at your sport. Today you choose how you are going to treat your teammates. Today you choose how you will love yourself, and yes, even how you will love God.

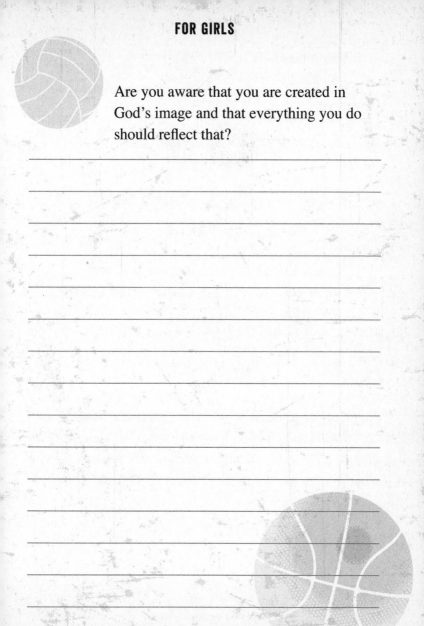

Are you aware that you are created in God's image and that everything you do should reflect that?

_____

_____

_____

_____

_____

_____

_____

_____

_____

_____

_____

_____

_____

_____

LOYALTY

**For I desire loyalty and not sacrifice,
the knowledge of God rather than burnt offerings.**

—Hosea 6:6

Loyalty is a great quality that coaches look for in their players. When a coach calls time out in a basketball game and draws up a play, she wants her players to execute the play and not to deviate from the set play. This is loyalty, doing what the coach asks in the heat of the game when things get tough. Loyalty means I can depend on you when things get rough. Be a loyal teammate. Be a loyal friend.

How do you demonstrate loyalty to your coaches and teammates?

_____

_____

_____

_____

_____

_____

_____

_____

_____

_____

_____

_____

_____

SERVANT LEADERSHIP

Whoever wants to become great among you must be your servant, and whoever wants to be first among you must be your slave.

—Matthew 20:26–27

Jesus was the most amazing leader there ever was. Yet His strategy was far different from the world's vision of leadership. He led by serving. Regardless of where you line up in the order of your team, you have the opportunity to serve your teammates. Serving may be in something as small as letting a teammate get a drink of water before you do or helping the manager after practice clean up. It tells the other person that she is important and special. Build someone up today.

How do you serve your coaches and teammates?

_____

_____

_____

_____

_____

_____

_____

_____

_____

_____

_____

_____

_____

KINDNESS

Love is patient, love is kind. Love does not envy, is not boastful, is not conceited.

—1 Corinthians 13:4

Kindness is not really what you think of when you think of an athlete, but this characteristic is very important to build unity and community among the team members. When you do not treat your teammates with kindness, bad attitudes can creep in and slowly destroy the closeness of the team. But when you are kind to your teammates, a bond of close-knit sisterhood starts to develop, and these teammates become friends you can trust. Love is patient; love is kind. Learn how to love your teammates by being kind to them.

Is your team close or are there bad attitudes that keep everyone from doing their best?

_____

_____

_____

_____

_____

_____

_____

_____

_____

_____

_____

_____

_____

_____

RENEWED STRENGTH

**Don't you know that the runners in a stadium
all race, but only one receives the prize?
Run in such a way to win the prize.**

—1 Corinthians 9:24

Whatever your sport, there are those practices, usually early in the season, when the coach is trying to get you in shape and you feel you just can't take another step. You have pushed your body to the limits and can't wait until you can rest after practice. Yet practice is not over. Pray for God's strength. He is not weary or tired and will give you the strength you need to make it through the practice and through the games. Pray for your teammates; that they too may have renewed strength and together you become a stronger, better team.

When you are tired, how do you get
through the rest of practice or the game?

TESTIMONY TO OTHERS

"Go back home to your own people, and report
to them how much the Lord has done for you
and how He has had mercy on you.

—Mark 5:19

As you get older, from time to time there will be opportunity for you to tell others about your game. Think of how professional athletes get interviewed immediately after a game. Usually these interviews are either all about the individual or the individual gives credit to God and his teammates. Realize that sports often offer a great opportunity for you to share with others about how much God loves you. Think about how much God has given you and, as the opportunity arises, tell others about it.

FOR GIRLS

How have you shared with your teammates
or others how much God has given you?

_____

_____

_____

_____

_____

_____

_____

_____

_____

_____

_____

_____

_____

JESUS' MIGHTY ENERGY

I labor for this, striving with His strength
that works powerfully in me.

—Colossians 1:29

Where does the power come from to see the race to the end and to finish with all the might you have within you? In a cross country race, a good course will usually have several hills to climb along the race. These hills seem to separate those who are just making it to the finish line and those who fight through the mental fatigue and finish strong. In this passage Paul tells us that the strength to finish the race strong comes from the Lord. Jesus gives you "His mighty energy," so finish strong!

Where does the power come from to finish
with all the might you have within you?

DON'T BOAST IN YOUR OWN SELF

For if I want to boast, I will not be a fool, because I will be telling the truth. But I will spare you, so that no one can credit me with something beyond what he sees in me or hears from me.

—2 Corinthians 12:6

Growing up my dad always told me that if someone was really good at their sport, they didn't need to tell anyone. Their actions spoke much louder than their words. He would also add that if someone had to tell you how good he was at his game, he probably wasn't that good. Be as good as you can be, yet no matter how good you are, have an attitude of humility within your soul.

Do you boast about how good you are or
do you show humility?

EARNEST COUNSEL

Oil and perfume make the heart glad, and the sweetness of a friend comes from his earnest counsel.

—Proverb 27:9

Some of the best friends you will ever have are those who you call your teammates. If you are playing soccer and your teammate is out of position, how do you tell her that she needs to get back in position? You can wait for the coach to correct her, but the coach may not have seen it. You may be the one that helps your teammate out by telling her of her mistake. Tell her about her mistake in an attitude of humility, not arrogance. You speaking to her humbly in love will deepen her respect for you and yours for her.

How do you respond when your friend makes a mistake?

_____

_____

_____

_____

_____

_____

_____

_____

_____

_____

_____

_____

_____

_____

APPROVAL OF MEN OR GOD?

**For am I now seeking the approval of man,
or of God? Or am I trying to please man?**

—Galatians 1:10 (ESV)

What motivates you to give your best or to win the game? Often you may find that you are really playing hard to please your coach, or your parents, or someone else. When you hit a shot in basketball, you quickly glance into the stands to make sure your parents were looking. Scripture tells us that you should be playing for an audience of one, Jesus Christ. The beauty of playing to please Him is that all He wants is for you to give your best and enjoy what you are doing.

What motivates you to give your best or to win the game?

_____

_____

_____

_____

_____

_____

_____

_____

_____

_____

_____

_____

_____

_____

CONTROLLING YOUR EMOTIONS

**A fool gives full vent to his anger,
but a wise man holds it in check.**

—Proverbs 29:11

The goal of an official is to see that the game is played on level playing fields, that neither team has an advantage over the other one on any given play. But the officials are human and will make mistakes. When they make a mistake (from your viewpoint), you have the option of losing control of your emotions and yelling at the official or showing self-control and not responding to her in a negative way. The Bible calls the woman who can control her emotions "a wise woman." Remember that officials are human beings, not just objects of the game you are playing. Treat them with dignity and respect.

How do you react to officials when they
make a call you don't agree with?

_____

_____

_____

_____

_____

_____

_____

_____

_____

_____

_____

_____

_____

Controlling Your Temper

**A fool gives full vent to his spirit,
but a wise man quietly holds it back.**

—Proverbs 29:11

Learning to control your tongue and your temper is a valuable lesson to learn in life. Sports seems to be the best arena to learn self-control and discipline. In basketball, because you are so close to the officials, you have to control your tongue when a call may seem to go against you or for your opponent. Regardless of how "bad" the call may be, you are required to respect the official and to keep your mouth shut, or you will find yourself getting a technical foul. God calls the woman who can control her tongue "a wise woman."

What things cause you to lose your temper?

INTEGRITY

**I know, my God, that you test the heart
and have pleasure in uprightness.**

—1 Chronicles 29:17 (ESV)

Uprightness here can also be translated *integrity*. It's been said that someone with integrity does the right thing even when no one is looking. Golf and tennis are the few sports where the player is also her own official. In golf, if you have to move your ball from its original spot, you are expected to penalize yourself a stroke even if no one else can see what you did. God knows the motives of women's hearts. He knows why you did certain things. Live before God as an honest woman who seeks to do His will all the days of your life.

Do you choose to be honest when no one else is looking since God knows all things?

BE STILL (TIME OUT)

**Be still, and know that I am God.
I will be exalted among the nations,
I will be exalted in the earth!**

—Psalm 46:10 (ESV)

In volleyball good coaches use their time outs to change the momentum of the game. A team will be on a roll, scoring point after point. The coach realizes it and uses her time outs to slow the other team down. The team circles around each other, and the coach looks them in the eye and tells them to pause for a minute, think about what they need to do, and then go back and do it. Often in life we need these "time outs" to pause, and refocus our thoughts, and then get back in the game. In this Scripture we are told to "be still" because we know that no matter what the day holds, our God is with us and will never leave us.

FOR GIRLS

Have you established a "time out" in your
day to reflect on God and your life?

_____

_____

_____

_____

_____

_____

_____

_____

_____

_____

_____

_____

BE TEACHABLE

**Listen to counsel and receive instruction
so that you may be wise later in life.**

—Proverbs 19:20

Are you teachable? Do you listen to the coach and do what she says, trusting that she knows more than you about the game and that she is going to direct you in the right direction? In practice a coach will go over a certain play time and time again. The coachable player is the one who listens and obeys the coach. But doing the right thing in practice is one thing. A coach is looking for that player who will do the right thing in the heat of the game when the temptation is to do her own thing. Learn to be teachable, a player that your coach can depend on to follow through with her wise instructions.

Are you teachable?

_____

_____

_____

_____

_____

_____

_____

_____

_____

_____

_____

_____

_____

_____

NEVER GIVE UP

**Therefore, since we have this ministry
because we were shown mercy, we do not give up.**

—2 Corinthians 4:1

Have you ever heard a coach say about a player, "She just never gives up"? What drives you to push yourself and never give up, regardless of what the scoreboard may say? Some games are going to be blowouts, and sometimes you may be on the winning team and sometimes on the losing team. When you are playing in a blow-out game, forget the scoreboard and continue to play as hard as you can. Don't let the scoreboard be the reason that pushes you to do your best. We continue to push ourselves because God's mercy never leaves us and leads us onward.

What drives you to push yourself and never give up?

_____

_____

_____

_____

_____

_____

_____

_____

_____

_____

_____

_____

_____

71

FAITHFUL IN SMALL MATTERS

For unless you are honest in small matters,
you won't be in large ones. If you cheat even a little,
you won't be honest with greater responsibilities.

—Luke 16:10 *(The Living Bible)*

When running sprints, it is very easy not to touch the line and hurry back to the next position. Coaches usually stand on the line to make sure everyone touches it. What is the big deal about touching the line every time? Does it really make you be in better shape? When you learn to be disciplined in the small things (touching a line in conditioning), it carries over in the big things. Be disciplined in the small things and the big things will take care of themselves.

What is your attitude about the small things?

_____

_____

_____

_____

_____

_____

_____

_____

_____

_____

_____

_____

_____

72

CHOOSING THE HARD ROAD

Enter by the narrow gate. For the gate is wide
and the way is easy that leads to destruction,
and those who enter by it are many. For the gate
is narrow and the way is hard that leads to life,
and those who find it are few.

—Matthew 7:13–14 (ESV)

Here the narrow gate can refer to the hard road. Everyday in practice there will be opportunities for you to take the easy way out—the short cut. But for you to be the best you can be, you need to push yourself through the difficult things and persevere though the road is hard. Afterward you will be glad you chose that path, and you will be a better person for choosing that road.

Do you always look for the easy way out
or do you see opportunities in the difficult
things?

_____

_____

_____

_____

_____

_____

_____

_____

_____

_____

_____

_____

_____

GOD IS OUR REFUGE AND STRENGTH

God is our refuge and strength, a helper who is always found in times of trouble. Therefore we will not be afraid, though the earth trembles and the mountains topple into the depths of the seas.

—Psalm 46:1–2

Are you ever afraid during an athletic event? If so, you probable have not performed at your best. The fear of failure prevents you from going all out. But, because God is your refuge and strength, you find in Him the strength to give everything you have to your event. Failure does not cripple you. Success does not define you. No matter what happens, God will never leave you or abandon you, so go for it with everything you have.

Are you ever afraid during an athletic event?

GOD GIVES US OUR VERY LIFE

**I lie down and sleep;
I wake again because the LORD sustains me.**

—Psalm 3:5

Every breath we have comes from the Lord. The arms and legs we have because God gave them to us. God made us just as tall as He wanted to, just as fast, just as strong. We take the body He has given us and, as we thank Him for it, we build it up to its maximum potential. Yet at the core of every workout we do, we know that God is the One who has given us our very life. So we are thankful to God for giving us the physical body He has that we may use it to bring Him glory. May you bring God glory by the way you play your sport.

Are you giving God glory by the way you play your sport?

_____

_____

_____

_____

_____

_____

_____

_____

_____

_____

_____

_____

_____

_____

_____

THE PRIZE

**Don't you know that the runners in a stadium
all race, but only one receives the prize?
Run in such a way to win the prize.**

—1 Corinthians 9:24

The tough thing about basketball and sports that end with a tournament or playoff is every team but one ends the season on a loss. Only one team ends the season with a win. So if your goal is the scoreboard, there is a very good chance that you will end your season very disappointed. The "prize" or "goal" should be to play with all your heart, to give the very best you can give. When you do this, you walk away from the season a winner and have peace in your soul, much more valuable than a trophy.

How do you feel about being the loser?

_____

_____

_____

_____

_____

_____

_____

_____

_____

_____

_____

_____

_____

_____

LOVED BY GOD

But God, who is rich in mercy, because of His great love that He had for us.

—Ephesians 2:4

How important is the scoreboard to you? Yes, it matters if you win or lose a game. One of the goals of the game is to out score the opponent. But don't let your self-worth or your self-esteem be caught up in the scoreboard of whether you win or lose a game. This verse tells us God loves us, not because we do well on the scoreboard or because we may be better than our opponent, but because of His great mercy, and Jesus dying on the cross, He loves us richly. Once we realize this truth, we are free to love others with that same kind of powerful life-changing love God has for us.

How important is the scoreboard to you?

_____

_____

_____

_____

_____

_____

_____

_____

_____

_____

_____

_____

_____

DIGNITY

**Strength and dignity are her clothing,
and she laughs at the time to come.**

—Proverbs 31:25 (ESV)

Dignity is the state or quality of being worthy of honor or respect. In sporting events, dignity often comes by the way you treat and respect others. In a close basketball game, the intensity of the game can cause you to see the opponent as the enemy. So the temptation is to treat her as "an evil that must be defeated." But your opponent is still a human being created in the image of God, just like you. Play to win. But in the heat of the battle, don't lose perspective of your dignity. Honor and respect even your opponent, and you will be known as a woman of strength and dignity.

Do you find ways to respect your opponents or are they "the enemy"?

INTEGRITY—SPEAK THE TRUTH

**The one who lives with integrity lives securely,
but whoever perverts his ways will be found out.**

—Proverbs 10:9

Are you known as a woman of your word? If your coach asks you to do something, will you do it regardless of whether she is watching you or not? In basketball the coach tells you to shoot 100 shots a day outside of practice and then to report back to her if you did or not. A woman of integrity will tell the coach the truth and accept whatever consequences may come as a result. Be known for a woman of your word. If you say you are going to do something, do it. If something comes up and prevents you from doing it, don't make excuses or speak untruthfully; just tell the truth.

Are you known as a woman of your word?

PERSEVERANCE

So we must not get tired of doing good, for we will reap at the proper time if we don't give up.

—Galatians 6:9

How many free throws do you need to shoot outside of practice to give you confidence to hit the shot in the game? How many serves to you need to make in practice to be ready to make the serve in the game? To become good at any sport it takes extreme discipline and practice, practice, practice. There will be days when it is very difficult to keep on practicing. But push yourself and keep working. Sometimes when running a marathon, the runners just have to speak to themselves and say, "Just one more step." And once you take one more step, you take the next, and then the next.

How much time do you spend practicing?

_____

_____

_____

_____

_____

_____

_____

_____

_____

_____

_____

_____

_____

GODLY DISCIPLINE

Have nothing to do with irreverent and silly myths. Rather, train yourself in godliness, for the training of the body has a limited benefit, but godliness is beneficial in every way.

—1 Timothy 4:7–8

When the Olympics come around every four years, we are able to hear story after story of how these athletes trained themselves to incredible limits to become Olympic athletes in their specific sport. The drive and determination to be the best that they can be is inspiring. This verse speaks of the value of spiritual training; spending time every day with the Lord in prayer and study. Often your discipline in your sport can carry over and help you be disciplined in spending time with the Lord.

Are you disciplined in training as well as spending time with the Lord?

_____

_____

_____

_____

_____

_____

_____

_____

_____

_____

_____

_____

_____

_____

FREE TO PLAY BECAUSE WE ARE LOVED

But from eternity to eternity the LORD's faithful love is toward those who fear Him, and His righteousness toward the grandchildren.

—Psalm 103:17

What difference does it make in the way you play if you know you are loved regardless of how you perform? This verse tells us that we are loved by God and He accepts us no matter how bad we may fail or mess up. Knowing that you can't fail should free you up to play with all your heart and not allow fear or rejection to prevent you from giving your all. You are free to "go for it," to try out for that team you didn't think you could make, to try out for that position you only dreamed you could get.

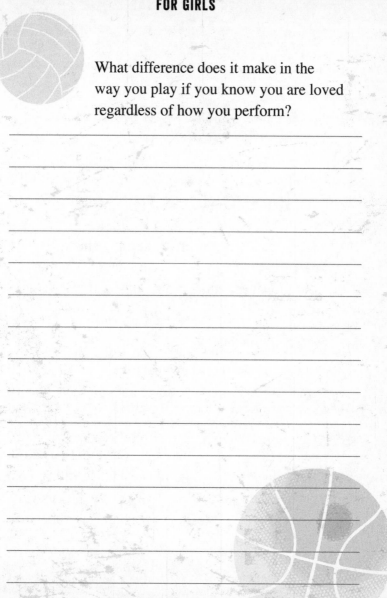

What difference does it make in the way you play if you know you are loved regardless of how you perform?

_____
_____
_____
_____
_____
_____
_____
_____
_____
_____
_____
_____
_____
_____
_____

CONFIDENCE IN THE LORD

The LORD is my strength and my shield; my heart trusts in Him, and I am helped. Therefore my heart rejoices, and I praise Him with my song.

—Psalm 28:7

When you go to the free throw line, do you have confidence that you are going to make the shot or do you believe that you will miss it? Where does your confidence lie? How do you gain confidence? Confidence comes when you know you are prepared for the task at hand and you have assurance that you can give your best effort. When you know that God is with you and He will be your strength and shield (protector), your heart is free and you have confidence to be able to give your all no matter what. You can play confidently.

How do you gain confidence?

_____

_____

_____

_____

_____

_____

_____

_____

_____

_____

_____

_____

_____

STIR ONE ANOTHER ON

**And let us consider how to stir up
one another to love and good works.**

—Hebrews 10:24 (ESV)

Have you ever had a teammate who builds you up so much it makes you want to play harder? When you look down the line of scrimmage and see a teammate who is giving her all, it inspires you to do the same. By ourselves it is easy to get stagnant and lose our motivation to move forward. But teammates encourage us to push on even when we think we don't have anything left. Be the player that encourages your teammates to play harder than they thought they could play.

Do you encourage your teammates to play harder?

_____

_____

_____

_____

_____

_____

_____

_____

_____

_____

_____

_____

_____

LOVED BY GOD THE FATHER

**And there came a voice from heaven:
This is My beloved Son. I take delight in Him!"**

—Matthew 3:17

This verse is when the heavenly Father is speaking about His Son, Jesus. It comes at the beginning of His public ministry; before He has done good "deeds" to earn His Father's favor. Jesus did not let the world define who He was. He knew He was loved by His Father and that is all that mattered. Do not let the world define you. Don't let your wins and losses define who you truly are. Don't let your failures or your successes define who you truly are. You are free to play as hard as you can because your self-esteem is not defined by your deeds, rather by God's love for you.

Do you feel like God will love you when you do good or do you know He loves you anyway?

_____

_____

_____

_____

_____

_____

_____

_____

_____

_____

_____

_____

_____

_____

SELF-CONTROL

Encourage the young women to love their husbands and to love their children, to be self-controlled.

—Titus 2:4–5

Have you every lost your temper during the game? Sporting events bring out our emotions, and when things don't go the way we want them to, sometimes those emotions come out negatively. Coach John Wooden (former UCLA coach) said, "Sports do not build character, they reveal it." It is impossible to be at our best if we are operating out of anger, rage, or frustration. Achieving self-control takes a lot of work and repeated practice. How do you respond to a bad call by an official? Each event is a test. Make a conscious effort to pass these tests by using good judgment and maintaining self-control even in the most challenging times.

FOR GIRLS

Have you every lost your temper during the game?

_____

_____

_____

_____

_____

_____

_____

_____

_____

_____

_____

_____

_____

177

RESPECT YOUR LEADERS (COACHES)

Remember your leaders who have spoken God's word to you. As you carefully observe the outcome of their lives, imitate their faith.

—Hebrews 13:7

The job of a coach is to make her players play better than they could play without her coaching. Coaches usually coach from their own experiences, learning from their own mistakes and failures. God is a God of order, not chaos. In His order He has set up the world with older people (coaches) who hopefully set an example by their word and their lifestyle of what they want their players to emulate. Therefore we are called to respect our coaches and obey their instruction, trusting that their instruction is for our good and the good of the team.

How do you respond to your coaches when they try to help you?

_____

_____

_____

_____

_____

_____

_____

_____

_____

_____

_____

_____

_____

ENCOURAGE ONE ANOTHER

Therefore encourage one another and build each other up as you are already doing.

—1 Thessalonians 5:11

The sport of volleyball demonstrates words of encouragement better than any sport I have seen. After every point, whether you win or lose the point, the girls quickly come together and encourage one another. If the teammate missed the shot, the words of encouragement challenge her to put that point behind her and get ready for the next point. If she made a great shot, the words of encouragement build her up to do it again. Learn how to be an encourager for your team, how to build up one another point after point.

Is there someone who encourages you to
do your best, and do you encourage someone else?

_____

_____

_____

_____

_____

_____

_____

_____

_____

_____

_____

_____

_____

TWO ARE BETTER THAN ONE

**Two are better than one because they have
a good reward for their efforts.**

—Ecclesiastes 4:9

Life is a team sport meant to be lived together. In team
sports like volleyball, basketball, soccer, softball, etc., the
object is for the team to be better than the individual. No
matter how talented a soccer player is, she cannot beat a
team by herself. Learn the value and strength of a team.
Learn to appreciate and accept the gifts your teammates
can bring to the team that you may not be able to bring.
Learn that the strength of two is stronger than the strength
of one.

How do your team members support and strengthen one another?

_____

_____

_____

_____

_____

_____

_____

_____

_____

_____

_____

_____

_____

_____

_____

PERSEVERANCE

You need to persevere so that when you have done the will of God, you will receive what he has promised.

—Hebrews 10:36 (NIV)

Many games are won by the team that can persevere until the end. Teams that are undisciplined tend to throw in their hat toward the end when the game gets intense. Where does this drive to be persistent to the end come from? Ask God to give you the strength to finish the game, to keep pushing yourself as hard as you can until the final buzzer. Keep focused on the task at hand; play your sport with all your heart. Then when the game is over, you can look back and know that you gave your best, regardless of the outcome.

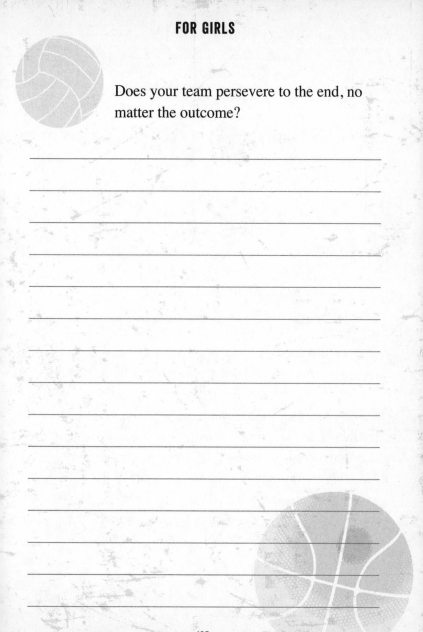

Does your team persevere to the end, no matter the outcome?

_____

_____

_____

_____

_____

_____

_____

_____

_____

_____

_____

_____

_____

_____

FORGET THE PAST

"Do not remember the past events, pay no attention to things of old.

—Isaiah 43:18

One of the hardest things to overcome in basketball is making a free throw when you have just missed the previous ones. In your mind you think to yourself, *I just missed the last few free throws and here I go again.* If your free throw was short, you have a tendency to overcompensate and make your next shot long. Your mistake of the previous shot can paralyze you from shooting the next one. Don't let a mistake in the past paralyze you from performing to your best in the present. Learn from your mistakes, but don't let them drive you to fear your present play.

How do you overcome your past mistakes?

_____

_____

_____

_____

_____

_____

_____

_____

_____

_____

_____

_____

_____

_____

_____

TWO OR THREE GATHERED

**For where two or three are gathered together
in My name, I am there among them.**

—Matthew 18:20

Being a part of a team gives you one of the most powerful opportunities to experience community and fellowship in our world. Think about how you can build up and encourage your teammate in your sport. It may be a pat on the back, a high five after a great play, or a word of encouragement after a point. It is a small way of saying to your teammate, "I am here with you. We are in this together and we are going to stand side by side through whatever comes our way this play, and the next." And as this verse promises, God is in the middle holding all of us in His strong hands and giving us the strength we need for the day.

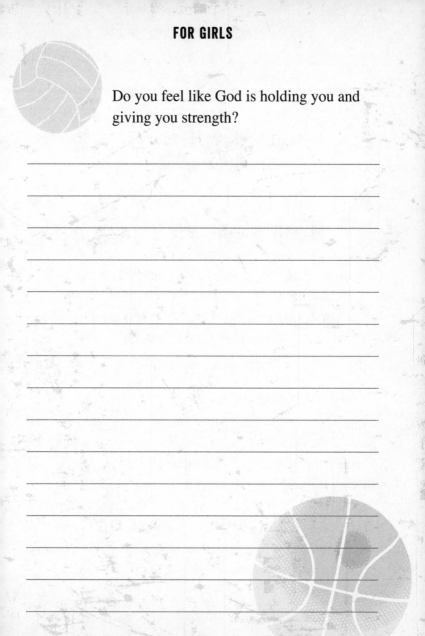

FOR GIRLS

Do you feel like God is holding you and
giving you strength?

_____

_____

_____

_____

_____

_____

_____

_____

_____

_____

_____

_____

_____

_____

92

REMEMBER GOD WHO GIVES ALL

You may say to yourself, "My power and my own ability have gained this wealth for me," but remember that the LORD your God gives you the power to gain wealth.

—Deuteronomy 8:17–18

To whom do you give the credit? On television after the game is over, the sports announcers usually have a post game interview with someone who made a difference in the game. Some of these interviews record the player sharing about how good she is, giving all her credit to herself. Then there are other interviews when the player shares that all the glory goes to God. God is the one who gives you everything you have. He gives you your next breath. So let's remember to give Him glory for all He has given us.

To whom do you give the credit?

_____

_____

_____

_____

_____

_____

_____

_____

_____

_____

_____

_____

_____

GOD MADE YOU

He is not impressed by the strength of a horse;
He does not value the power of a man.
The LORD values those who fear Him,
those who put their hope in His faithful love.

—Psalm 147:10–11

What can you do to make yourself taller? What can you do to make your eyes a different color, or your hands bigger? No matter how hard you may work, there is nothing you can do to add an inch to your height, or change the color of your eyes, or make your hands bigger. God made you exactly the way He wanted, and God doesn't make mistakes. Never lose sight of the fact that you are His creation, that you are fearfully and wonderfully made, and He holds you in the palm of His hands all the days of your life.

FOR GIRLS

What can you do to make yourself taller?

_____

_____

_____

_____

_____

_____

_____

_____

_____

_____

_____

_____

_____

No Grumbling or Complaining

Do everything without grumbling and arguing.
—Philippians 2:14

In life you are going to be asked to do things that you don't want to do. In your sport, your coach will ask you to do things that are not fun and exciting but that usually are crucial to make you and your team a better team. When you are asked to do these things, your attitude can make all the difference in the world. A poor attitude will criticize and complain, whereas a positive attitude will uplift and encourage your teammates. The easy thing to do is to grumble or complain. But what God asks of you is to do all things without grumbling or complaining.

What kinds of things has your coach asked
you to do that you didn't like?

_____

_____

_____

_____

_____

_____

_____

_____

_____

_____

_____

_____

_____

_____

PATIENCE

Be patient until the Lord's coming. See how the farmer waits for the precious fruit of the earth and is patient with it until it receives the early and the late rains.

—James 5:7

Patience has so much to do with sports. You want things to happen instantly, but often it takes time for things to develop. In basketball, coach calls time out and draws up a well designed play that entails players must wait for their time to enter the play. Once the play begins to develop, the players patiently wait for their time to enter the game. In life, often it takes time for things to develop. So we wait for the Lord, but our waiting is active, not passive.

Where can you practice having patience?

GIVE A HELPING HAND

If you see your brother's donkey or ox fallen down on the road, you must not ignore it; you must help him lift it up.

—Deuteronomy 22:4

Have you ever fallen down or been knocked down so hard that someone had to help you up? This simple command in the Bible is telling us to help each other up when we fall down. In basketball, when a player takes a charge, her teammates hurry to her and help her up. They do so because she just made a selfless play that helped the team. But in games and in life, we will get knocked down and our friends will get knocked down. Be that friend today who is helping up your teammate when she is knocked down. Give her a helping hand.

FOR GIRLS

Have you ever been knocked down so hard
that someone had to help you up?

_____

_____

_____

_____

_____

_____

_____

_____

_____

_____

_____

_____

_____

_____

WOMAN OF NOBLE CHARACTER

Her sons rise up and call her blessed. Her husband also praises her: "Many women are capable, but you surpass them all!"

—Proverbs 31:28–29

What is in a name? When someone calls your name, what do they think? In this passage the author is describing what a godly woman looks like on a daily basis. You are making a name for yourself by the way you practice and by every game you play. What is the name you are leaving? Will they remember you as a player who gave her all every time she hit the court, or will they remember you as someone who had great talent but never really maximized her talent? Give your all every time you play.

FOR GIRLS

When someone calls your name, what do they think?

_____

_____

_____

_____

_____

_____

_____

_____

_____

_____

_____

_____

_____

_____

TO WIN THE PRIZE—TO KNOW GOD

**I pursue as my goal the prize promised
by God's heavenly call in Christ Jesus.**

—Philippians 3:14

Every four years when the Olympics return, we watch incredible stories of dedicated athletes who have gone to extreme measures of training to achieve the prize, which is a gold medal. At the beginning of every season, you make goals for yourself and for your team, then you set out with discipline and determination to achieve those goals. In the above verse Paul has set a goal: to know Jesus Christ. He keeps going every day with that goal in mind. Press on today with the prize in mind of getting to know and love your heavenly Father more and more.

FOR GIRLS

What goals have you set for this season?

_____

_____

_____

_____

_____

_____

_____

_____

_____

_____

_____

_____

_____

WORK HARD AND LEAD

**Work hard and become a leader;
be lazy and never succeed.**

—Proverbs 12:24 *(The Living Bible)*

Who are the leaders on your team? Who are those girls you look up to and you are counting on to come through when the game gets tough and someone needs to make a play to win the game? True leaders have earned the right to be called "leaders" by their work ethic in practice and off the field in their life. God has given you the physical body you have. Everything about your body is a gift from Him. So working hard in practice is a way of saying "thanks to God for what He has given you." There is nothing stopping you from being that leader. Your team is always looking for girls to step up and lead by your example. So go forth and lead.

Who are the leaders on your team?

_____

_____

_____

_____

_____

_____

_____

_____

_____

_____

_____

_____

_____

PLAY TO THE GLORY OF GOD

If anyone speaks, it should be as one who speaks God's words; if anyone serves, it should be from the strength God provides, so that God may be glorified through Jesus Christ in everything. To Him belong the glory and the power forever and ever. Amen.

—1 Peter 4:11

Why are you playing sports? There needs to be a reason that goes deeper than yourself. Hopefully you are playing because you enjoy the game and all that it brings to you. But as Christians we are here on this earth for something much greater than just enjoying life. We are here to live life in such a way that it really brings glory to the God who made us. We are here to shine the light on Jesus. The way we play our sport has the awesome opportunity to shine the light on God.

Why are you playing sports?